Body Language

How to Understand and Talk to Any Person

William Muller

and audio unless express consent of the Publisher is provided beforehand. Any additional rights reserved.

Furthermore, the information that can be found within the pages described forthwith shall be considered both accurate and truthful when it comes to the recounting of facts. As such, any use, correct or incorrect, of the provided information will render the Publisher free of responsibility as to the actions taken outside of their direct purview. Regardless, there are zero scenarios where the original author or the Publisher can be deemed liable in any fashion for any damages or hardships that may result from any of the information discussed herein.

Additionally, the information in the following pages is intended only for informational purposes and should thus be thought of as universal. As befitting its nature, it is presented without assurance regarding its prolonged validity or interim quality. Trademarks that are mentioned are done without written consent and can in no way be considered an endorsement from the trademark holder.

Table of The Contents

Introduction 5

Gaining A Deeper Understanding 7

Being Aware of Your Own Body Language 11

Main Guidelines for Reading 18

People 18

Eyes 30

Ears, Nose, Cheeks, Jaw, and Chin 37

Mouth, Lips, Smiles, and Laughter 41

Head, Neck, and Shoulders 50

Hands, Including the Palms, Fingers, and Thumbs 58

Arms and Touch 68

Chest, Torso, and Belly 73

The Position of the Body and Its Role in Body Language ... 76

Body Language and Lying 81

How To Use Body Language To Your Own Benefit 86

Reading the Body Language of A Child 93

Conclusion 103

Introduction

In this book, we are going to look at how we can use body language as a means of communication in order to convey the meaning that we truly want to transmit to others.

Reading and utilizing body language are two of the most important skills anyone can learn in order to function in the real world. In fact, body language is so important that it plays a significant role in our lives without us even realizing it. The reason for this is that much of our body language is subconscious.

By the same token, many of the interactions that we have with others around us also happen at a subconscious and even instinctive level. There are times when we don't stop to pay attention to what is happening during a social interaction, yet the message is loud and clear. Many times, that message is sent without a word being said.

This book is ideal for anyone who is looking to improve their communication skills at a non-verbal level. It isn't some book intended to show you "cheats" or "hacks" for communicating with other people. Rather, it is about building genuine interaction with other individuals in such a way that you can truly get your message across and thereby achieve your personal goals and objectives. As you hone these skills, you will find that you will also be able to build meaningful relationships that will help you feel more confident and fulfilled.

So, come on in. Let's find out how you can make the most of the skills you already possess by putting them into perspective non-verbal communication. You will find that becoming a master communicator is a lot easier than you might have thought.

See you on the inside.

Gaining A Deeper Understanding

When we talk to the people closest to us, we want to understand what they are truly trying to say. If they are discussing a difficult situation, we do not want to miss an important detail that hasn't been explicitly stated. If we are in a serious discussion with our spouse, we do not want to miss a cue that could mean they are upset with the way we are speaking. If you are talking with a child about how great they did on their sports team that day, we want to make sure that all of our excitement strikes a chord with them.

These are all important details to notice in conversations. Unfortunately, we cannot notice or portray all of these details with words alone. Our bodies will help us to discuss and share our emotions whether we want them to or not. Through body language, our conversations gain a deeper level of understanding. Being able to read body language will ensure that you are able to get this level of deep understanding correct and that you will be able to use what you learn in your conversation or relationship.

First, when looking into this topic, it is important to note that things are not always as they seem. If a person is telling you that they love you, but they do not have a happy face, your first instinct may be to think that they are lying. In reality, they may be tired. While this example seems rather obvious, the fact of the matter is that most folks say a lot more with their facial expressions than with their words.

Another important thing to consider is that if you are saying one thing and you feel differently, your body may betray your true feelings. For instance, I have seen many individuals claim to love someone, yet they are unable to look at them in the eyes while they say it. In fact, you might see some folks

look down as they say this. Of course, this might be a sign of submission, but it is also a sign that they may be lying.

Based on this example, it is clear that the body language that you use will affect the people you are surrounded by. Your body language could show them that what you are saying is true or it could show them that what you are saying is a lie. Your body language could also show them that you are nervous or uncomfortable, happy, or excited. Typically, your body language will show the people you are speaking to how you actually feel. If they are able to read these cues, they will be able to read straight through your words and into how you actually feel.

On one occasion, I found myself having to give a speech in front of a small group of people. While I have never been particularly shy, I was a bit nervous since this was the first time I was delivering this particular speech.

So, I stood up in front of my audience and introduced myself. I then proceeded to rifle through roughly 45 minutes of material in about 20. While I had thoroughly prepared my notes and rehearsed what I wanted to say, I found myself speaking like a machine gun.

After the speech, one of the audience members walked up to me and said, "You were a bit nervous, weren't you?" I replied, "Yes, a little. How did you know?" My initial expectation was for her to say that I had spoken to fast. Her reply surprised me: "you stood up there like you had roots in the floor".

What?

Roots on the floor?

Then it hit me: I had not moved at all during my speech. I just stood there, with my index cards in my hands, and just rifling away.

You see, comfortable and relaxed people speak with their hands and move in a natural, free flowing manner. By just standing up there like a statue, I had made it rather obvious that I was nervous as could be.

This is why I like to recommend folks to observe themselves when they speak.

You can take a look at yourself in a mirror or have someone else videotap

you. The idea is that you need to see yourself. That is the best way in which you can gain a third-party perspective on the way you handle yourself when speaking and attempting to communicate with others.

Being Aware of Your Own Body Language

It is not only helpful to be able to read the body language of the people around you, but it is also important to be able to read your own body language. This can be a difficult task because it's not always easy to see yourself from a third-party perspective. That is why I recommended that you observe yourself in a mirror or even through video.

To be able to read your own body language, you need to be extremely aware of your body and the ways in which it moves. You need to be so aware that you can feel the slightest movement, like the slightest movement of shoulders or legs. You even need to be aware of the movements your body does not do in a specific situation. For example, you might not be making proper eye contact thus making a conversation a bit awkward.

Being aware of your own body language can be difficult, but it is an extremely important skill to acquire. In this chapter, we will look into some things that your body language may be telling the people around you. By being able to get a handle on your body language, you will be able to line up your words with your actions and movements.

Your Body Language May Tell

Perhaps the most common reason people become interested in reading others through their non-verbal communication is to determine when a person is lying. The so-called "human lie detectors" are not gifted individuals who have innate abilities. While they are certainly clever folks, they have simply mastered reading people.

For example, they are very much familiar with eye contact and eye movements. One telltale sign of a lying individual is the lack of eye contact. However, you can still pick up on lies even when an individual makes a point of not looking at you. You can easily pick up on this if your interlocutor has "shifty" eye movements, that is, if they move their eyes from left to right, as if to see if there is anyone coming after them. This eye movement is an involuntary response that can be a signal that something's up.

Your Body Language May Make Others Feel Good About Themselves

Your body language can actually have very positive effects on the people that you are talking to. If you are touching the person, smiling, laughing, and looking at them more than usual, you may give them just the boost of self- esteem that they may be looking for. Of course, touch is something you need to be careful with as unsolicited touching can get creepy very quickly.

That being said, facial expressions such as smiling, or open gestures such as holding your arms out when speaking can go a long way toward making others feel much more comfortable around you. These types of behaviors will signal to your counterpart that you are receptive and willing to engage them in a forthcoming manner.

One other important aspect to consider is called "mirroring". When you act in a similar manner as your interlocutor, you appear to be "in synch" with them. What this does is that it creates a pattern in which your counterpart feels comfortable, as if you "get them" at a subconscious level. While we will be getting into this into greater detail later on, it is worth mentioning that you can implement this today by simply observing that the other person is doing and behaving accordingly.

Your Body Language May Make Others Upset

If you are doing the opposite of the things listed above, your subtle actions could have the exact opposite effect. If you keep a distance, do not smile, do not laugh, do not make eye contact, or simply do not pay much attention to the person you are talking with, you could actually make them feel uncomfortable. Also, your tone of voice plays such an important role in helping others feel comfortable around you. So, do take the time to make sure that your voice is signaling what you are really feeling at any given time.

Your Body Language May Confuse Others

Many types of body language are easily understood by the people around us. If we smile at them and stand close to them, they probably feel that we are happy spending time with them and like who they are as a person. If we ignore the person and talk to them without even looking at them, they will feel the negative tone. If your body language does not match up to how you are feeling or if it is very inconsistent, you may confuse the people around you.

For instance, have you ever encountered a colleague that shakes your hand without looking at you? How does that make you feel? Does it seem like this person in uninterested in you or perhaps even dislikes you? If you have ever been in this situation, you can appreciate how a lack of eye contact can convey a negative message.

Conversely, what if there was a colleague whom you genuinely disliked, but you still looked at them and smiled at them often? Would that convey your true feelings? Perhaps you are just being polite in order to spare that person's feelings. Nevertheless, you might be subconsciously sending conflicting messages as other aspects of your body language may give away your true feelings.

I recall one occasion in which two colleagues who disliked each other greeted one another at a conference. They were both very polite and professional. However, their displeasure for one another become painfully evident as they gave each other a weak handshake despite smiling and exchanging cursory pleasantries. Needless to say, it got awkward rather quickly.

So, if you want to avoid having your body language confuse the people around you, you need to be aware of it and make sure that it matches with how you feel and how you are trying to portray yourself.

One other common situation in which your body language can send mixed signals is in the dating world. When you look at smooth-talking individuals who are looking for love, you often see them talking up the right game, but they completely lack the non-verbal communication to go with it.

Some smooth talkers have the lines down right, but they don't maintain healthy visual contact, they don't keep a healthy posture and even resort to creepy and cringeworthy touching. In fact, you may even find that some so- called dating gurus tell their followers to touch early, and often, so that the other party can get the message that they are interested.

I'll say this again: unsolicited touching can be creepy right away and derail your chances at making a genuine connection with someone in a matter of seconds.

That is why you need to pay attention to how you conduct yourself. If you show good posture, smile like a normal person would, and respect your interlocut0r's personal space, you will have a great chance at hitting things off without seeming like a creepy fella.

Your Body Language Can Make You Seem Confident

Body language, facial expressions and gestures in general can be a dead giveaway for confidence of lack thereof. When you are confident, your mannerism will send that message. For instance, confident individuals have square shoulders and look straight ahead. While drooping shoulders may simply be bad posture, the fact of the matter is that your posture will reveal far more than you think.

In order for your body language to portray confidence, you need to be keenly aware of the ways in which you move and behave. You need to take powerful body language movements and incorporate them into your day. It can be difficult to change something that is barely noticeable, but it is certainly a helpful skill to master.

A good rule of thumb to keep in mind is to be aware of how your body language lines up with your intended message. If you genuinely like a person, then make sure that your body language matches your words. Also, if you genuinely dislike a person, make sure that your body language does not offend that individual. After all, there is nothing wrong with being polite.

Main Guidelines for Reading People

In this chapter, we are going to be presenting six main guidelines which you can take into consideration with regard to non-verbal communication and body language as a whole.

Guideline #1: Do Your Homework

Students of human behavior and psychology know the sources which they can rely upon to get updated information on the subject. Now, you ought to be careful with the sources that you consult since there is plenty of information out there from sources claiming to be legitimate. And while much of that information is rather straightforward, you need to take it with a grain of salt. This is especially true of those self-proclaimed gurus who claim they have unlocked the secrets to human behavior and so on.

Academic sources such as the Journal of Psychology and Behavioral Science runs quarterly reviews on literature and publishes studies which can provide you with up to date information on topics that may be of interest to you.

Also, the Open Access Journal of Behavioural Science & Psychology is a solid, peer-reviewed publication that presents research on topics pertaining to psychology, behavior and human nature in general.

In addition to the classics of psychology such as Freud and Jung, experts such as Harvard psychologist Jordan Peterson often publish highly popular YouTube videos and academic articles which present psychology and behavioral science in a digestible and easy to process manner.

Guideline #2: Men and Women React Differently To the Same Stimuli

Males and females, while perfectly equal from a biological perspective, are hardwired differently from an evolutionary perspective. This goes all the way back to the days in which men were predominantly the hunter-gatherers while women were tasked with the domestic tasks of providing care for infants and the home.

As such, this evolutionary cycle has led

men and women to view things
entirely differently. So, women tend to be more agreeable than men thus seeking to avoid conflict as much as possible. On the other hand, men tend to be more disagreeable and prone to engage in conflict. This is why men tend to be more aggressive than women. While there are plenty of

aggressive women out there, men tend to play the role of warrior far more often than women do.

Of course, modern society has done its best to breakdown traditional paradigms and strive for equality in terms of gender roles. Nevertheless, the fact remains that both men and women look at things from clearly different angles. This is why it's important to have a clear understanding of what is permissible behavior among men and women.

For instance, consider proxemics. If a man stands too close to a woman, this might be construed as "creepy" since it is a violation of personal space. Likewise, unsolicited touching and contact can even lead to potential sexual harassment claims. Hence, the "arm's length" rule is a great way of avoiding a violation of personal space. Furthermore, refraining from physical touching, unless invited, is the best course of action that can be taken to avoid misunderstandings and inappropriate behavior.

Guideline #3: We Are "Programmed"

This is a common misconception. For starters, there are many folks who believe we have all of our behaviors and instincts hardwired into our DNA. Therefore, there is not much we can do to change that.

While that is partially true, the fact is that a great deal of our behaviors are learned through the cultural influence of our families and social groups. As discussed earlier, most of the behaviors, gestures and mannerisms we exhibit on a daily basis are learned. That is why we can try out best to adopt the behaviors that we feel will best help us foster effective communication with others. In a sense, we can "deprogram" much of the program which was given to us from our upbringing and conditioning in childhood.

Guideline #4: There Is No

"Silver Bullet" To Reading People

You will often find individuals claiming to know all the secrets to reading people. In fact, many will claim they hold the one secret to reading people's minds. Granted, these claims are often found in the dating world. Many of these experts claim that they have mastered the art of reading. So, all you need to do is buy into their program and you will have everything you need.

Now, it is true that there are techniques that can unlock your understanding of people's true feelings, the fact of the matter is that there is no "silver bullet". You cannot realistically expect to have one super Jedi mind trick that you can use to understand people. The reality is that this is a skill which is comprised of various smaller skills.

For example, you must learn to decode body language, facial expressions, tone of voice, and so on.

Consequently, your journey to reading others like a book the result of your concerted effort to learn individual clues and how these clues all line up at once. As you gain more proficiency, it will seem like it's one super-duper trick when in reality it is a collection of strategies rolled into one system.

Guideline #5: Age Plays A Key Role

While we will be going into this in greater depth later on, it goes without saying that dealing with children is far different than dealing with elderly folks. Children, especially younger kids who cannot verbalize their feelings quite as much, will give off loads of non-verbal clues as opposed to elderly folks who are far more communicative.

As such, it is important to pay attention to children's actions and gestures. For example, pouting is a classic sign of displeasure. Nevertheless, crying can have a host of meanings.

As for adults, the myriad of feelings that can conflate into single actions can certainly be challenging to decipher. Even then, younger adults will act out in certain ways as opposed to older adults who may show far more restraint.

This is largely due to generation differences predicated mainly on culture. Generally speaking, newer generations have become somewhat laxer on expressing feelings as opposed to past ones. Nevertheless, the underlying, subconscious mannerisms remain the same.

Guideline #6: Context Is Key

In addition to gender and age, many factors about the conditions surrounding a body language reading can change its meaning: where you are, why you are there, your relationship with the person, any conversation you were just having, the person's personality, and so on. It is important for you to take into account any information about context that you have available to you, or else you run the risk of entirely misinterpreting someone's body language.

For more information on how context can influence readings of a person, please check out my other book, *Speed Reading People*, where I go into the topic in detail.

Perhaps the biggest takeaway from this last guideline is that experience will teach you best. In that regard, your observations will become your biggest ally in understanding and decoding the non-verbal and contextual clues that folks around you give off at all times.

In the next section, we are going to learn the specifics of reading people. And if you like what you've learned so far, or you've found benefit, feel free to leave a review on Amazon. I really appreciate it as your feedback means a lot to me.

Facial Expressions – Face and Forehead

When you think about body language, one of the first things that come to mind is the face. Whether you are thinking of smiles, frowns, raised eyebrows, or a mouth held tightly shut, there are many emotions that can be portrayed through facial expressions.

One of the most important things to know about body language that stems from the face is that it is the easiest type of body language to fake. Most people are very aware of their face and the expressions that they are making. Because of this, they can choose the right type of expression or movement that they need to convey meaning to their interlocutors. However, they would like to be seen. It is important that you know this so that if a person's overall body language is not adding up, it could be fairly likely that they are faking their feelings through their face.

Eric Ravenscraft, in his 2014 article called, "How to Read Body Language More Effectively", published on lifehacker.com, speaks of emotions that are commonly faked through the face. The first one that he mentions is fake

smiles. He says that in most cultures, children are taught from a young age that they are supposed to smile in certain social situations. This teaches the children whether or not their smile is real; it should be on their face during these times.

For example, imagine you open up a Christmas gift from your beloved grandmother. It is a sweater that she knitted especially for you. It is a color you have never worn in your life and it feels quite itchy even when you are simply running your hand over it. This makes you realize how much worse it will feel when you actually put it on.

How do you react when you open this box? Do you allow your face to portray the negative emotions that you are feeling toward the sweater? Typically, our answer to this question would be "no." In this situation, we know that our grandmother loves us and worked hard on the gift that she made for us, so we fake a smile and act like we love it.

This fake smile portrays to the people around us that we are happy with the gift, even if we are not. This is an experience that most people have gone through in their life. You may, however, just be realizing that in times like this, you have been causing the people around you to misread your body language through facial gestures that do not match up with how you are really feeling.

Luckily, with the right information, it is actually

possible for us to tell if the people around us are smiling for real or if they are using this fake smile. To tell the difference, study a person's face closely when they are smiling. With a real smile, our eyes and sometimes even our whole head is involved. We may raise our eyebrows or look slightly upward while the edges of our mouth come up to form a smile. In a fake smile, it is only the mouth that is moving at all.

The study of facial expressions and their meaning goes much deeper than just smiles. As shown in Paul Ekman's aforementioned book, he and Wallace Friesen popularized the reading of facial expressions in 1978 through a system called Facial Action Coding System (FACS).

In FACS, Ekman and Friesen identified each area of the face and head through labels. Each one of these areas has movements that line up with specific emotions or feelings. These movements can be slight and barely noticeable, or they can be large facial gestures and expressions.

FACS is typically used by trained people in the field. This technique has been done by computers and can be performed on certain types of monkeys, like chimpanzees. It can even be helpful in the diagnosis of disorders such as depression.

In FACS, the amount of facial movement is recorded. These movements can be A (Trace), B (Slight), C (Pronounced), D (Severe), and E (Maximum). Such movements include eyebrow-raising, eye movements and forehead creasing.

On the subject of forehead movements, one of the biggest things to look at when studying the body language of the face is the forehead. A wrinkled forehead, for example, can mean that a person is surprised. A sweat covered forehead can mean that they are nervous or afraid. If the person touches their forehead, it can mean they are stressed or that they are trying hard to figure something out.

Indeed, facial expressions play a significant role in understanding a person's feelings despite what their words are actually attempting to convey. The main thing to keep in mind is that body language is much more than just facial expressions. So, keep an eye out for other clues. Consequently, facial expressions are just the tip of the iceberg when it comes to studying non-verbal cues.

In general, facial expressions are the first impression you get from a person. While arms, hands, posture and even fidgeting all play a significant role, it is facial expressions that hit us first. Also, facial expressions are the hardest to cover up. Most people are unable to disguise their facial expressions as they are generally the product of subconscious reaction. So, using a "top-down" approach, that is, starting from the face down, you can gain a leg up on reading people.

Eyes

Our eyes are extremely expressive and are often considered to be one of the most useful tools in body language. Because of this, there is a lot to learn when it comes to reading them. Our eyes can tell many things, from movements that we can control to movements that we are unaware of. In this chapter, we will look into what these movements are and what they mean so that you are able to read them in your own life.

One of the most interesting body language cues that the eyes have comes from the pupils. This is because we have no control over our pupils, what they do, or how they may move. We all know that pupils get smaller or larger depending on how much light we are around, but pupils can actually also dilate when we are interested in the person we are talking to or the thing that we are talking about. If you see a person's eyes dilate during a conversation and the light around them has not changed, it's likely that they are genuinely interested in the interaction that is happening. It could also indicate that the person is aroused. The same goes for if you see that person's eyes open wider as well. In direct opposition to that, if you see a person's pupils constrict and/or they start to squint without a change in external stimuli like lighting, it could be an indicator that they dislike or disagree with something in your conversation or something they see in your surroundings. It could also mean that they are concerned about something or have perceived a potential threat. Nevertheless, it is best to remain calm and cross-reference other non-verbal clues in order to confirm pupil dilation as a legitimate non-verbal clue.

Another form of body language that comes from the eyes that we do not really control is blinking. We can control our blinking, of course, but it is often done without us even noticing. Since blinking is an involuntary movement, it may let on more that we'd like to.

Visual contact is one of the most important means of non-verbal communication that we can learn to decipher and to master. Visual contact is essential in both professional and personal relationships.

For example, when I meet someone for the first time, I like to shake their hand and look them square in the eye while I smile. In a professional setting, this will make it clear that you are confident and relaxed.

On a personal level, visual contact through direct eye contact is a great way to show you are interested in a person. This is often taught in the dating world though care needs to be taken in order to avoid being creepy. The fact of the matter is that friendly eye contact will help you signal potential romantic interest so long as your visual contact is directed at a person's eyes and not some other part of their body. Of course, it is important to avoid staring at the other person for prolonged periods of time. Also, blinking regularly will make eye contact much more natural.

Additionally, eye contact can mean that a person is interested in talking to you or that you are the subject that they are talking about. When a person is genuinely interested in you, they won't hesitate to make eye contact. In fact, they may very well put their phone away. If this is the case, then you know you have really hit the mark with this person.

Conversely, a lack of eye contact can also mean that a person is uninterested in you or, at the very least, what you have to say. They could be easily bored by the conversation or just not really committed to carrying the talk to its end and they could be using a lack of eye contact as a sign to show you this.

Strong, consistent eye contact can also mean that a person is trying to seem powerful. Oftentimes, you may feel intimidated by this strong type of stare. It is a way that people can purposely show the power that they believe they have over you. This type of body language is actually believed to be primal since dogs can become afraid or aggressive if they feel threatened by your consistent eye contact.

Consistent eye contact can even mean that a person is lying to you. This may seem counterintuitive as a lack of eye contact is usually taken as a sign of mistrust. However, if a person is aware of this, they might make it a point to look at you when they speak. Yet, there is a point when this visual contact is unusual or awkward. At that point, you can infer that this individual is hiding something, but they are trying to convince you they are not.

Of course, a person's natural reaction is to look away when they are lying. This is an involuntary response as they feel shy or insecure. Even master deceivers will make this mistake at some point. This is why interrogators look at suspects straight in the face until they break in some manner.

Nevertheless, a lack of visual contact doesn't always mean that a person is lying to you. It can simply mean that they are nervous or shy. This is especially true when you are engaged in a situation such as a date or even a job interview. In such cases, your interlocutor might simply be nervous and overwhelmed. It is possible that, overall, the person is not comfortable with making eye contact, even if they are not particularly nervous or shy. Such discomfort can stem from their upbringing, their culture, or if they have a specific disability such as autism. This is why I always try to make folks feel comfortable by looking at them in the eyes and then give them a chance to look away.

Another interesting thing to look into when discussing the body language that is spoken by eyes is the direction in which a person points their eyes. Another element to keep in mind is that if a person points their eyes to their left, they are trying to remember an event of the past. If a person points their eyes to the right, they are trying to be creative and come up with a new idea.

Rolling one's eyes is another common, though often involuntary, form of body language expressed through the eyes. When it is not done intentionally, rolling one's eyes typically indicates annoyance, disagreement, or even boredom. It is common among teenagers to the point that it is part of the teen stereotype to roll your eyes often. However, adults do it as well. No matter if it is due to annoyance, disagreement, boredom, anger, or what have you, if you see someone roll their eyes and it is clearly not on purpose, you can take this as a sign that they are not telling you something and it is probably negative.

Body language that has to do with eyes can also include things that we do purposefully. For example, we may sometimes communicate through winking, which is a form of body language. We may also silently ask for help from someone around us through crying when it is too hard to ask with our words. People can also cry to get the things that they want in an unfair manner. These are not heartfelt tears but rather they are a manipulative device. Hence, they receive the name of "crocodile tears". We might also purposefully roll our eyes at someone, either because we do not particularly care for them and/or what they are saying or because we are teasing them and rolling our eyes in a playful manner.

It is clear that eyes play a significant role in communicating meaning. Nevertheless, the usual suspects like pupil dilation, blinking, eye contact, winking, movements and even crying may not be enough to ascertain what a person is feeling. Other clues such as paying attention to how far open a person's eyes are may let one far more than you think. For instance, movie directors depict suspicious characters by narrowing their eyes while cheerful and hopeful characters generally have wider, more open eyes.

Ears, Nose, Cheeks, Jaw, and Chin

The body language that is shown by the face is deep and can portray an endless amount of different feelings and emotions. In this chapter, we will look into how body language can show through the ears, nose, cheeks, jaw, and chin. We will look into what these movements mean and how you can read them on others and on yourself.

First, let us look into ears and how they can speak to us. Most commonly, ears relate to body language with an action called ear pulling. This causes the person to either lightly pull on, wipe their hand over, or slightly block their ear. This could be done because a person is lying or when they are feeling stressed. They perform this body movement because their ears get extra blood sent to them which in turn causes them to be red and uncomfortably hot.

Max Atkinson, in his 1984 work Our Master's

Voices, points out that certain

gesticulations such a touching nose or ears may indicate that a person is lying. The main point behind this assertion lies in the fact that involuntary movements are triggered when a person is subconsciously nervous or hiding something. Consequently, such movements may be seen as a comfort mechanism rather than part of a person's behavior.

Next, let us look into the cheeks. Cheeks seem like things that do not move and that really would not be able to say much, but there are a few different things that they can portray. When cheeks are sucked in with a person's breath, for example, it can mean that they do not approve of what is going on. When a person blows their cheeks out, it could mean that they are trying to make a decision or that they are very tired.

As we know, cheeks also often turn red in certain situations. This can be a useful tool when you are trying to read body language through their cheeks. This redness can mean that the person is angry or embarrassed. You would be able to tell the difference between the two based on another body language that happens at the same time. If cheeks lose their redness altogether, on the other hand, it might be a sign that the person is feeling ill for one reason or another.

Moving on, the chin is actually a very interesting part of the body to learn about when it comes to body language. If a person is holding their chin inward, it could be a primal instinct that suggests that they are feeling threatened or being submissive. This is because holding the jaw in this position can protect the throat. If a person pushes their throat outward, it could mean the opposite. It could be a sign of dominance or a sign that the person wants to fight. If a person's chin is in neither of these two positions and is more so held flat, it means that they feel safe and not at all threatened.

Sometimes, even the beard that a man decides to grow can affect their body language. If a man has a full beard that he simply let grow without any fancy keeping, it shows that they are comfortable with who they are naturally. If their beard is full and messy, however, it could mean that they simply do not care about their appearance or it could show that they are going through a hard time in their lives. A beard can let you know if someone participates in the rules of their own culture as well.

Conversely, sometimes people run their hand over their jaw. This typically means that they are deep in thought. If a person puts their hand under their chin to help hold up their head, it usually means that they are tired but also may mean that they are bored.

It is amazing how such small features of the face can have such a wide variety of meaning when it comes to body language. Typically, these parts of the face tend to go unnoticed. With the information that you have learned in this chapter,

you will not only notice their movements, but
you will be able to understand exactly what they
mean as well.

Mouth, Lips, Smiles, and Laughter

We typically see the mouth as part of our body that speaks, but usually, we focus on the fact that it speaks words. In reality, our mouth speaks at a much deeper level than the simply verbal version that we hear every day. Our mouth plays a huge role in body language and nonverbal cues as well.

If you have ever talked to someone who could read right into you and who always knew how you were feeling below the surface, they may have spent a great deal of time staring at your mouth during your time conversing together. Experts today actually believe that the best readers of body language tend to look more at the mouth of the person they are reading than anything else. The best place to look was previously thought to be the eyes, though now the consensus is that the mouth is the best place to focus on.

Typically, people breathe through their nose, so if you see someone who is breathing through their mouth, (and it is not due to a full-on stuffy nose!), this could teach you something about how they are feeling. If a person is breathing through their mouth, they are trying to take in more oxygen than usual. This could mean that they are scared or that they are so angry that their body is preparing them for a fight response. However, it might simply mean they have a breathing problem which restricts their air intake. So, do pay attention to these potential issues in order to avoid misreading signs.

If the person is breathing quickly through their mouth, it could mean that they are undergoing large amounts of stress or that they are having a panic attack. It could also simply mean that they are too hot and that their body is taking in more oxygen in an attempt to cool them down.

If a person is breathing quickly but not deeply or loudly, they may be extremely sad. This is a good cue to pick up on if someone is in need of support but is too embarrassed or depressed to reach out to the people around them.

Deep breathing can also have many meanings behind it. Deep breathing into a yawn could mean that a person is sleepy or that they are finding boredom in the situation or conversation that they are participating in. Deep inhaling and exhaling with closed eyes could show that a person is trying to calm down or relax their bodies. Long, deep breaths followed by a sigh could mean that a person is sad, bored, or even frustrated or angry with what they are doing.

Also, something as simple as your lips, which serve various purposes independent of communication, can serve as a means of communication. For example, when someone presses their lips outward in a tight circle, it can often mean that they are not comfortable with the situation or conversation that they are in. Going back to Ravenscraft in his article "How to Read Body Language More Effectively", looking for this lip movement is actually a way that experts analyze the speeches and confessions of politicians. They can tell if the speaker is talking about something that they are not comfortable with or some that they possibly do not believe is true through this trick.

Pursing one's lips can also reveal something about the person who is doing it. Sometimes, pursing the lips means that someone is thinking, either about what was just said or about something that they want to say. It could also indicate that the person is displeased, annoyed, nervous, or hesitant. This gesture can often occur during an awkward pause in a conversation as they try to think of if and how they should proceed with the discussion.

If someone licks their lips, it could be because they have a desire for something that they are seeing or thinking about. This desire can be as simple as a desire for delicious food that they see or smell. However, it can also point to a more sexual desire for the person with whom they are speaking. Be careful with this interpretation, though, as licking their lips could also just be the person's subconscious act of trying to moisten uncomfortably dry or chapped lips.

Smiles, of course, come from the mouth and have significant meanings within the area of body language as well. As we mentioned earlier, smiles can be real or fake. A real smile will light up a person's whole face including their eyes and even their eyebrows. A real smile may also cause a person's whole head to lift up. A fake smile has only to do with the person's mouth. Smiles, of course, mean that a person is happy if they are real. They can mean that a person feels satisfied with the conversation or that they are even proud of you when they are talking to you. Smiles can also mean that a person is interested in you and interested in getting to know you better. Another interesting fact to note is that fake smiles last longer than real smiles. With this information, you should be able to tell the difference between both fake and real smiles and this will help you to know what a person means by the body language that comes with a smile.

Let us look into different types of smiles. A half smile is a smile that is only using half of the face. This often means that a person is not necessarily happy but sarcastic or not sure of how they are feeling. It can also mean that a person is nervous but is trying to look confident in what they are doing.

Soft smiles can be considered submission to some. They could mean that a person is shy or that a person is showing you that they are not trying to compete with you.

In some cultures, smiles might have a different meaning than in other places around the world, although the variations are few and far between. Sometimes a smile can mean that you have a question to ask. Other times it can mean that you have something to say and you are waiting to be called on.

Smiles are not the only thing with the mouth that body language reads into. We can also look into what it means when a person is not smiling. A person who holds their mouth tightly shut could mean that they want to say something, but they are trying not to. This could be if they're upset, but they are trying to act like a nice person. It could also mean that they have something to say, but it is not appropriate to say at that specific time. Also, if a person has their mouth in a straight line and their eyes are not looking very kind, it can mean that the person is upset or judging the people about them.

Of course, a lack of smiling can also lead to frowning. Frowning is a sign that a person is sad. It could mean that they feel bad about what you are saying or that they have something hard going on in their own lives.

An open mouth with wide eyebrows and eyes can mean that a person is surprised or shocked at what they are hearing or seeing. This can be a good emotion or a bad emotion, and you will need to look at the other body language signals that the person is showing off to tell between the two.

When we look beyond the shapes that a mouth can make, we often think of the sounds that it makes. We are not talking about words here because this is about body language; we are talking about laughs. Laughing shows that a person is happy and that they are enjoying themselves. They think that the thing that was said is funny or that what they see is funny. Laughing is often a short thing and does not take much time. However, there are many different types of laughs.

A person may laugh a lot when they are embarrassed or nervous. This laughing may make them feel at ease or take their mind off of the difficult situation that they are about to face or that they just finished facing. This laughing may seem inappropriate for the time, but it is the person's way of coping. It is important to know this type of body language so that if someone is laughing out of an uncomfortable place, you are able to help them. They may be too embarrassed to ask for help, but your knowledge of body language will help them to avoid the not need to ask. You will simply know what to do to help them.

Indeed, laughter can be considered to be a positive emotion especially when seen in light of attraction. Women actually tend to laugh at men who they like, and men love to be laughed at. Because of this, laughing in an early relationship is a good sign that the connection between the two people is strong.

Sometimes, we may laugh when things are not necessarily funny. We may laugh when others get hurt or if we see things that are not in a video but are somewhat relatable to us. This is probably not actually because the things we are seeing are funny, but because we are uncomfortable and laughing is our body's response to making the situation feel better. It is important to know that this type of laughing is different than laughing at funny things so that we do not get upset with people for laughing at things that should never be laughed at.

Type of body language that stems from the mouth is when people suck on their hand or bite their fingernails or other things when they are uncomfortable. This often starts in early childhood as a comfort mechanism but may come back to adults and older children when they are extremely uncomfortable. If you see a person doing these things, they are likely nervous and may need someone to support them. They probably do not like that they have to engage in these behaviors, but they are hard to stop because they allow the person to feel comfortable again. If you see a person that is sucking on their thumb, try not to judge them. It is something that they may need support for and that they would likely benefit from a person being on their side. It is important to note that biting means that a person is in even more stress than if they are sucking. This knowledge will help you comfort people who are nervous or uncomfortable when you come across them. It will also help you to know if you have a habit of biting your nails or sucking your thumb, that is just common and that it is not something you need to be embarrassed about. It is something that you may be able to change if you help yourself to feel comfortable in your own life and the situations that you enter.

As such, a keen understanding of body language is so powerful that it can enable you to help others and not just yourself. Most importantly, this keen understanding will allow you to take much of the guesswork out of human interaction. This is so powerful since you will be able to help others feel comfortable especially when it is obvious, they are not. Understanding how the mouth works is one important element in reading people. Yet, the are other parts of the body which still need to be discussed such as the head, neck and shoulders.

Head, Neck, and Shoulders

We have talked about the body language of the face and each body feature that is on it. Next, let us take a look at the head as a whole. We will also move down into looking at the body language that comes from the neck and the shoulders.

First, we will examine what it means when a person lets their head hang lower than normal. If a person lowers their head but their eyes are still looking up at you, it is likely that they feel you somehow serve as a threat to them. This threat can mean that they have an automatic response to fight you, whether this fight—and the perceived threat that caused it—is physical or not.

If a person lowers their head and has their eyes toward the ground, though, it can mean that they are afraid or are submitting themselves to you. It is possible that they think that you might hurt them, or they might just think that you are much more powerful than they are. It can also mean that they think you are a wonderful person and that you are so great that they can't even look at you.

This particular gesture can also indicate that the person is embarrassed or ashamed. They could also be feeling guilty about something. When someone hangs their head and looks at the ground, they might be trying to avoid any possible eye contact with you. Why they are doing it, however, depends heavily on what you had been discussing beforehand. If, for example, you had just been talking about a naked baby picture of theirs that their mother had shown you, they could be embarrassed by that picture. If they had just finished telling you about the time that they were put in detention for cheating on a big math test, they might be feeling a bit ashamed by that mistake, no matter how long ago it was. If you were talking about something of yours that went missing, it could mean that they actually took it and feel guilty about having done it. The guilt version of this gesture might even occur the moment that they see you, in which case, you might want to be on alert for receiving bad news from this person.

Also, if a person puts her head down and is not making one of these specific body language cues, it could just mean that they are extremely tired. Heads are a happy part of our body as we all know and if we are extremely tired, it is hard to hold our heads up.

When a person puts her head down quickly, it could mean that they are ducking or hiding from something that they think is coming toward them. This could be something that really is coming towards them like a ball at a sporting event or something that they are imagining in their head.

Nodding of the head could also simply mean that the person is nodding yes. Often this means that the person is saying yes to you, but it could also mean that they are simply acknowledging your presence. It is often a positive sign that the person is interested in your presence.

Now, let us shift gears to what it means when a person holds her head up high rather than lowering it. If someone raises their head, it could mean that they are following something that they are interested in so that they do not have to look away from it. It could also mean that they are simply interested in what they are seeing if they tend to raise their eyebrows with their head as well.

If a person puts her head up in the air and stares upward for a long amount of time, it could mean that they are extremely bored or tired. This would mean that they are not interested in anything around them enough to look at it and that they are ready to move on to something else. If the person is not bored, it could mean that they are trying hard to focus on something that they are hearing. They may feel that the things that they are seeing are distracting them from what their ears are hearing and that they need to look straight up into nothing to be able to hear the best that they can.

In the opposite way, if a person puts their head up quickly and shortly, it could mean that they are not into you. It could mean that they are giving you the go-ahead to do something or that they are asking you what you mean because they are confused.

When a person is not tilting their head up or down but rather to the side, it could mean that they are interested in what you are saying or in what is happening around them. It also means that they are very attracted to you if they look at you in this way. This is because tilt in the head means that they are curious and want to learn more about what they see. If a person is attracted to you, they often want to get to know you better and the tilting of the head is a good sign that this is true. If a person tilts their head just a little bit, they might be self-conscious or not sure of their actions, but if they tilt their head a great deal, it means that they are extremely interested and curious of what they are looking at.

Of course, most cultures agree that nodding one's head up and down means that they are saying yes. Typically, shaking one's head from side to side means that they are saying no. These are easy to read signals that you have probably been able to read since you were young.

Not all body language is so easy to read, however, so this chapter should help you in your quest to understand it better. Now, we will also look into the body language that is shown by a person's neck.

When a person is constantly touching their neck, it can often mean that they are stressed or embarrassed. It could mean that they are worried as well. If someone is rubbing their neck, it could mean that they are embarrassed, but it might also mean that they are angry or frustrated and that they are trying to calm themselves down with the gentle pressure. This is often why it is suggested to give someone a neck rub when they are feeling stressed. We know inside of us that this is a helpful tactic. Remembering this tactic when you are reading body language can be extremely helpful. Even though it is something that most people know instinctively, it is something that is good to remember and easy to forget.

Of course, it is important to remember that some gestures of touching one's neck, such as rubbing or scratching it, could be nothing more than a reaction to pain or an itch. Just like the gentle pressure can alleviate stress, it can also alleviate tension or a knot in the neck that is causing pain, so the person could easily have a stiff neck rather than be mad at you or frustrated. That is why it is crucial to take context, such as the conversation you are having when this motion occurs, into consideration when reading body language.

Is also important to note that when a person protects their neck with either of their head or their hands as it means that they are feeling threatened. The neck is a vulnerable place as it can be injured easily and seriously, so when a person protects it, it means that they are trying to protect their life.

Let us look at what it means when body language comes from a person's shoulders. When a person holds her shoulders high, it could mean that they are afraid or if they are excited. If a person hunches their shoulders and holds their arms close, it could mean that they are cold because this helps him to warm up.

If a person scrunches their shoulders forward in front of their body, it could mean that they are feeling defensive or that they are afraid. It could also mean that they are trying to hide from something that scares them. If they do the opposite and push their shoulders back, it shows that they are ready for the fight that they believe is about to happen. It could also mean that they are confident and believe that they are about to succeed.

When a person is moving their shoulders in a circular fashion, it could mean that their shoulders are sore or that they are trying to relax their body after being nervous. This relaxes our shoulders and the muscles within them, so if a person was holding their shoulders tight previously, this could help them to relax afterward. It could be a sign that they just went through something difficult and that they are trying to get back to their normal selves.

Take a simple gesture like shrugging. This gesture might mean that an individual does not know the answer to a question which has been posed, or it could mean that they simply do not care. Partial shrugging or shrugging just one shoulder can show insecurity or a lack of commitment on that person's part about whatever is being discussed. It might also mean that the person is being evasive and/or deceptive regarding the conversation, and so it could be taken as a sign of lying. A person who shrugs a lot when they are not talking could also be lying. In general, it is easier for them to just remain silent rather than to try and verbally express the lies and remember every detail of it, so

excessive shrugging could be their attempt to communicate without stumbling over their own lies.

When you relax your entire body, it is often seen

that our shoulders are one of the first things to relax. If you relax your shoulders, it is hard to tense up any other type of body part. This means that if you see a person with very relaxed shoulders, they are probably very stress-free and relaxed themselves.

The head, neck, and shoulders can be great indicators of body language and how a person is truly feeling. The movements that these body parts do can tell you a lot about the person's situation and now that you know the signs, you should be able to read into the signals in your real life as well.

Hands, Including the Palms, Fingers, and Thumbs

Hands are something that we often do not look at or pay much attention to when we are speaking to another person. Have you ever heard, though, of how much you can tell about a person based on their handshake? This is due to the body language that hands portray. In this chapter, we will look into hands as well as that famous handshake theory. We will also look into the smaller parts of hands including the palms, fingers, and thumbs.

We have mentioned a little bit about hands throughout the book so far as we have been working towards learning body language together. We have looked into the fact that when people touch certain parts of their body with their hands, it can mean certain things. But the hands actually have much larger of a role in body language than just touching noses and ears. The hands are complex body parts with many bones, and they can do many things that relate to our emotions.

First, let us look at what it means when we hold things in certain ways. If you hold a container or cup with gentle hands, it could mean that you consider the object special or fragile. It could also mean that you were trying to give it to someone as a gift. If you hold the object extremely tightly, however, it could indicate exactly the opposite. It could mean that you want to keep the object and that you are not very careful with it. However, it could also mean that you are nervous or afraid of dropping the object.

As per Hanneke K.M. Meeren's 2005 study, hands play a significant role in communicating meaning to other individuals [1]. For instance, the way in which a person holds an article may be an indicator of their inner feelings. This can be seen in defensive positions such as folded arms indicating self- protection. Open arms, on the other hand, might indicate a more open, welcoming attitude.

Also, you can look at the tightness of a person's grasp or just the way that a person holds their hands to tell how stressed or upset they are. The tighter that the person holds their hands, the more upset or stressed they are. People often take out stress by squeezing which can be seen through this.

When the person is holding their hands, it can actually mean much more than what we have previously discussed. If a person is gently holding their hands together behind their back, it allows their shoulders to open up and allows their posture to be better. This helps to show that the person is confident and believes that they are able to succeed at whatever task they are about to do.

If the person is holding their hands in front of them, however, it can mean the opposite. When someone clasps their hands in front of them, a side effect is usually that their shoulders will roll forward, thus closing off the person's chest from whomever they are speaking with. This can be a sign of a lack of confidence, especially if they also do not hold their head very high. However, it could also be a sign of submission to the other person or even a sign of shyness or other discomfort as they try to close themselves off as protection from a potential threat.

Also important to note is that people who are lying are trying to make sure that their hands are not moving. This is a way that they try to control their body language, but you might actually be able to see that they are controlling it and tell that they are lying through their efforts.

There are times when you can tell that a person is nervous because their hands are constantly moving. When they are clicking a pen or tapping on a table, this can mean that they are nervous or stressed about something that is about to happen. If you see someone who is nervous in this way, you might be able to offer your support.

Conversely, someone who is nervous might also hold their hands in an attempt to keep them from moving so frantically, much like when a person is lying. This can often lead to another gesture, i.e. the wringing of someone's hands, that is a well-known tell of when that person is anxious.

Often times when people are happy, they also speak with their hands. If a person is moving their hands largely while they are speaking and are smiling and using bright eyes, it is probably because they are happy and excited about the topic that is being discussed.

Of course, not everyone talks with their hands because they are nervous, happy, or excited. Some people talk with their hands just because it is how they are. They might be naturally energetic and moving their hands when they talk might be part of how their body releases this energy. Maybe they regularly use sign language to communicate with someone who is deaf, and so it feels natural to them to move their hands a lot when they are talking even when they are not using sign language. It is also possible that this is just quirk of theirs, perhaps something learned from watching a parent or other adult move the same way while they were growing up. Like all body language, talking with one's hands can mean a lot of things, so it is necessary to take context into account before jumping to any conclusions.

If someone is touching another part of their body with their hands, that can also hold certain meaning, as we already saw when we talked about someone touching their neck. Touching a specific part of the body while talking with someone can be seen as an attempt to draw attention to that body part with the reason varying based on which body part the person is touching. For example, if a woman touches the inside of her wrist repeatedly while it is visible to the other person, it could be a sign that they are flirting with that person. This interpretation of this movement is based on the fact that the inside of the wrist is a part of the body not often exposed to others and, thus, to show it is an attempt to show some vulnerability. By touching it, the woman is trying to draw attention to the fact that they are showing the other person some vulnerability, thus expressing a desire to be more intimate with that person.

Of course, sometimes touching a body part could just be a subconscious gesture stemming from some discomfort in that area. For instance, someone rubbing their eyes could mean that something, like dirt or an eyelash, is stuck in it and causing itchiness. It could also indicate that the person is tired. Someone touching or rubbing their temple might indicate that they have a headache, although it could also mean that they are irritated or exasperated with either you or the conversation the two of you are having. When sitting down, rubbing or running their hand over their knee could show that their knee hurts. However, it could also be a nervous habit that reveals that the person is uncomfortable with their current environment, company, topic of conversation, or overall situation.

The meaning behind using one's hand to touch other body parts is as varied as people's personalities and personal quirks. Nevertheless, there is usually some sort of meaning behind the gesture. If you are familiar enough with that person and their personal ticks, you should be able to decipher exactly what this body language means for this person and determine from there how you should proceed.

Next, let us look into the palms of the hands and how they play a role in body language. Palms seem like a small thing that could not have much meaning behind them, but that is not true.

Let us first look into what it means when a person holds their hand out with their palm facing up. As such, an upward facing palm means that the person is trying to get you to cooperate with them. According to Meeren (2005), it is said that even monkeys like chimpanzee use this gesture when they need support. The gesture helps those around you to see that you are peaceful and that you are equal to them. It shows that you need help and that you are requesting it in a calm and happy way [1].

When you face your palm toward the ground, it can mean the opposite. It can show that you want to be in control of the conversation or that you would like other people to be quiet. It can also be a way to stop people from interrupting you as you try to speak. It is often a way to tell people to stop or wait.

Next, let us look into the body language that can be read through fingers. The most common ways that fingers are used in body language is by pointing. Everyone knows what pointing means, and it often means the same thing throughout different cultures. Finger-Pointing can show someone where something is, or they can allow a person to call on someone else. However, it can also be considered rude, especially when you're pointing directly at someone, so you have to be careful with where you point and the intensity with which you do so.

The position in which someone holds their fingers can also speak volumes as to a person's attitude and attention level. One prominent example is a gesture called the steeple. In this gesture, the fingertips of one hand press lightly against the fingertips of the other in a way that mimics the steeple of a church, often while being held up in front of one's chest. Sometimes, this gesture includes a motion of the palms moving back and forward, giving the appearance of a spider doing push-ups on a mirror. When this gesture is done with the fingertips pointed up, it is usually a sign of the person's confidence. It can even convey an overconfidence, perhaps even smugness and arrogance or a feeling of being above the person that they are speaking with, as the prayer-like image attempts to project a God-like façade. This particular form of the gesture is referred to as the raised steeple.

The lowered steeple, though, carries a much different meaning. While it still indicates a level of importance, steepled fingertips pointed downward mean that the person is paying attention to whatever their conversation partner is saying. This form of the gesture makes the user look more interested and ready to respond. Even though both men and women use the lowered steeple, it is actually more common to see women doing it.

The raised steeple and the lowered steeple are perfect examples as to why you must pay attention to every detail of body language in order to execute an accurate reading. After all, you do not want to mistake someone as being smug just because they are using steepled fingertips when, in fact, their hands are in the lowered steeple position. Even the slightest change in position can change the entire meaning of someone's body language.

Thumbs can be used in a similar way to fingers. The position of a person's thumb is an especially good indicator as to their confidence level. In general, people carrying their thumbs high signals that they have high confidence. Someone putting their hands in their pockets with their thumbs sticking out, particularly when they are a high-status individual, displays a high confidence level as well. Similarly, a thumbs-up often means that the person is confident, that you are doing a good job, or that that person is having a positive experience. Thumbs down, on the other hand, often means that something is going bad.

Some thumb positions also indicate that someone has a low confidence level. For example, when someone sticks their thumbs in their pockets with their fingers dangling outside of them—a reverse of sticking their thumbs out of their pockets—it can mean that they are unsure of themselves or feel uncomfortable.

As you can see, gestures can say a lot more than you intend to at a conscious level. This is why it is of the utmost importance that you consider the importance of paying attention to your behavior and mannerisms. In doing so, you will be giving yourself the opportunity to communicate exactly what you wish to say while avoiding mixed signals.

Arms and Touch

Touch is one of the most controversial forms of communication. For some folks, touch can be a powerful means of communicating feelings and emotion. It can signal something very deep and meaningful between two individuals. For others, it might be seen as uncomfortable and even frowned upon in their culture. Consequently, it is important to take a deeper look at how touch and the use of arms can be utilized effectively in communication.

First, let's look into the body language that

comes from arms.

If a person opens their arms wide, it can mean that they are friendly towards you. It could mean that they want to hug or that they are happy to see you. It could also mean that they are upset with you or want to start a fight. You will be able to tell the difference between these two things based on the other body language that you see taking part with arms.

Arms can also be used to make certain shapes. They can show a person details of a conversation that cannot really be explained. You can use your arms to show someone how big something is, or you can use your arms to demonstrate a specific action. Arms can also show a person details of a conversation that cannot really be fully explained by the use of words. Arms are a powerful aspect of your body language. As such, they can drive your point home or sink your message.

Yet, properly managing your arms is one of the most important skills you can learn in non-verbal communication as it displays sincerity. In general, people
tend to trust others who use their hands when speaking since it shows that they are truly engaged in what they are saying.

On the contrary, folks who do not use their hands when speaking seem robotic and insincere. While this may just be the effect of nerves, it does not give off a vibe of sincerity. As such, these folks may simply come off as being insincere or uninterested in what they have to say.

Furthermore, arms can also be used for waving, as a means of saying hello, or they can be used to wave as a signal of danger. If you raise one arm up into the air, it might mean you have a question. If you raise both your arms up into the air fast, it could mean that you are frustrated or that you are confused.

Arms may even be used in a threatening manner. You can use them to attack a person, or they can be used in imaginary fights to show what you are capable of doing. They can also defend you if someone tries to fight you. They can block a person from hitting or hurting you.

If you cross your arms in front of your body; it often means that you were uncomfortable or scared. This is almost similar to forming a shield in front of your body to protect yourself.

If you reach your arms forward, it could either mean that you want to be close to the person near you or that you are trying to attack the person near you. This difference can be told by how fast the movement is and by other body language features that accompany it.

Now, if you should happen to hide your arms behind your body, it could mean that you are comfortable and that you trust a person near you. This shows that you do not need your arms to protect you and shows that you are happy in the situation that you were in. However, it might also be misconstrued as an indication that you have something to hide, hence, you have put your hands behind you back. This is why it is always important to have your hands out in front of you at all times.

I would also like to make one additional point on arms. Over time, open hands, palms facing upwards and other "open" gestures with your hands and arms indicate friendliness. One such example of this is the military salute.

Virtually all militaries throughout the world
have some type of salute in
which they face they allies with an open hand in
front of them. The salute can be similar to the one
used by the United States armed forces in which
a soldier's palms are facing down, or it could be
like the British salute with the open palm facing
forward.

Whatever the variation of the salute, it is a clear
example of how this gesture is taken to mean
friendliness. In the Middle Ages, friendly knights
would pass each, and in order to indicate they
were allies, they would take their right hand off
their swords and use their open hand to lift up the
visor of their helmets. This allowed friendly
knights to both make direct eye contact and show
that they meant no harm.

To this day, any type of open-palmed gestured is
taken to indicate friendliness and non-aggression.
So, it certainly pays for you to pay attention to
this when you interact with folks. Whenever you
see hands opening up, you can infer they are
friendly and comfortable around you. Any time
you see a fist coming up, then you can take that
to mean a sign of aggression or defensiveness.

When considering touch, it is important to keep in mind that all types of touch need to make sense at the time they happen. For example, a hug given when a person is upset and needs comforting makes sense. Otherwise, unwarranted touching can lead to a person feeling uncomfortable. This may lead to rejection and potential accusations of impropriety.

Also, it is important to keep in mind that the "arm's length" rule is the safest way to go. In addition, it is worth noting that friendly touch such as a tap on the shoulder or light touch on the elbow can help create a friendlier interaction. However, this is dependent on the level of familiarity among the parties. So, it is best to limit physical touch to handshakes with people whom you are not familiar and escalate touch as interaction permits. It is simply best to avoid touch when you are unsure of whether it would be deemed appropriate or not.

Chest, Torso, and Belly

The chest, torso, and belly make up the midsection of our body. This part of our body is hard to move on its own so it seems like it would not add much to our overall body language. However, this part of our body actually does have a lot to see. In this chapter we will look into these things in detail.

If a person pushes their chest outward, it is often a sign that they are attracted to you. Women do this to show their breasts, and men do this to show how strong they are. If it is not a sign of attraction, it could be a sign that someone is showing dominance over you or is simply feeling confident in themselves and in their abilities. Of course, in trying to show their dominance over you, the person might also be issuing a challenge or a threat, but that can only be determined with the help of other body language signals and context.

When a person does the opposite and pulls their chest inward, it means that they are feeling afraid or vulnerable. People might do this if someone tries to attack them or if they simply feel threatened by a certain situation. This adds into what we talked about earlier with curling forward your shoulders. People often do these two body language things at a time.

The chest also plays a big role in leaning forward. People often lean towards other people when they feel attracted to them, when they are interested in what they are saying, or when they want to be close to them. They might also, however, lean toward someone when they feel power over that person or when they want to show dominance over that person. You will be able to tell the difference between these two things by the other body language that the person is portraying.

We mentioned breathing earlier, but the chest can exaggerate the body language associated with the act of breathing. When a person breathes in in a certain way, it is seen through their chest, so looking at the chest is a good way to tell if a person is breathing in a specific way.

Next, let's look into how the torso plays a role

in body language.

Form of body language with the torso happens when a person touches their stomach. A person may touch their stomach if they're not feeling well after eating too much food. They could also touch their stomach if they are feeling stressed or worried.

The person is pulling in their stomach and it may mean that they want to look attractive and they feel overweight. If a person is pushing their stomach out it could mean that they feel comfortable or that they feel vulnerable and want some space. You will again be able to tell the difference between these two things by the other body language that the person is showing.

The chest, torso, and belly might not be able to move much on their own, but they do play a large role in body language. After reading this information, you should be able to tell what a person is trying to say through the movements that the middle section of their body makes.

The Position of the Body and Its Role in Body Language

In this chapter, we will be taking a look at the role the entire body plays, through movement, in transmitting knowledge. While we have discussed individual body parts, such as arms, it is also important to see how the entire body can be used to convey meaning to others.

First, let's look into what our legs have to say. A person uses their legs in many ways throughout the day. When they're standing, their legs might say certain things about how they are feeling. If a person stands with their feet apart, it means they feel comfortable in the situation that they are in and they feel confident in their abilities. If their legs are spread wider than shoulder width apart, it means that they are trying to find a powerful position in the group. If their legs are close together, it could mean the opposite. It could mean that they're worried that they are in a dangerous situation. If a person is standing with their legs open, it makes the genitals more visible, and it could be a sign that the person is attracted to you. If they stand with their feet not next to each other but instead with one in front of the other, this could mean that they are feeling unsafe and are preparing for an attack. It could also mean that they have a plan to go somewhere and they want you to follow.

Next, we will look into the body language of the buttocks. If a person pushes out their bottom, it could mean that they find you attractive. In other situations, it could be an insult. You will be able to tell the difference between these two things based on the other body language that the person is portraying.

A person is moving their bottom; it means that they are trying to draw attention toward it. This is often meant to bring people in, and it's not an insult in most cases. This is often done in dances to attract people of the opposite gender.

The previous example illustrates how dance is a means of non-verbal communication meant to transmit a specific message. In fact, many cultures throughout the world is using dance as a mating ritual. Certain types of dance are used to signal availability. Such dances can range from upbeat rhythms such as those seen in some African tribes to swanky balls thrown by courtiers. In either case, dances are often used to communicate at a primal and instinctive level.

Another important aspect to consider is stance, be it when sitting or standing. For instance, if you sit with your hands on your knees and your back straight with your feet flat on the floor, it means that you were paying attention and are interested in what the person has to say. However, if you slouch over and look like you're about to get up, you do not look interested in you look like you want to leave the conversation.

If you sit with your back storage down so far that your elbows are able to touch your knees and your hands are able to bend up and hold your head up, it means that you do not want to talk to anyone. It means that you may be stressed or upset, and you want to be left alone.

If you sit with your back turned to the point that you can put your elbows on your knees and your hands are simply laying limp in front of you, it means that you may not have the confidence in you that will allow you to do what you were trying to do. if you sit with your back bent to the point that you can put your elbows on your knees and your hands are simply laying limp in front of you, it means that you may not have the confidence in you that will allow you to do what you were trying to do. It means that you feel like you are not able to succeed, and you are accepting fate.

Next, let's look into some standing stances. You stand with your arms behind your back, but with one arm grasping your other arm, it means that you are angry. This could be a primitive reflex to stop yourself from hurting or punching another person. If you stand with your arms crossed in front of your chest, that means that you are maybe feeling threatened or you are simply uncomfortable in the situation that you are in. If you slouch your body with your arms hanging and you're back far from straight up, it means that you were tired, or you are upset with your poor performance that day. If you stand with your arms by your side and your hands clenched in first second me that you were very stressed out or anxious about something that is about to happen. If you stand with your hands relaxed and together in front of your body, it can mean that you are in control of your body and that you are comfortable in the current situation.

Stand with your arms bent at an angle and your fist sitting on your hips; it means you are ready for what is about to happen. It could mean that you are confident in your abilities or that you are simply ready to try. If you stand with your arms at your side but your hands and fingers loosely laying on your legs, it means that you are friendly and ready to go. It means that you are not stressed and that you are open to what is about to happen. It also means that you may be a friendly face for people to come up and talk to. The stance is inviting and comforting to the people around you.

There are many different ways to stand or sit with your buddies, but these are some good places to start. Do your stances tell you how your body is portrayed to others as well as help you understand how others are feeling based on the way that their body is held. If you understand these dancers, you will be able to read people simply by the way they are standing or sitting.

Body Language and Lying

It can be difficult to tell if someone is telling the truth or if they are lying. Luckily, there are ways to help you figure out the answer to this question. Body language is a great tool in figuring out if someone is telling the truth or lying. It is often even used by professionals and people in the jails and court systems to tell if criminals are innocent or guilty. In this chapter, we will tell you how to look at a person while they are speaking to tell if they're lying or telling the truth.

First, we will look into what it means if someone pulls on their ear. Typically, when people are lying, they may rub or pull their ears. This is done to make sure that they are getting blood flow to their ears and to control their body temperature. Blood flow and body temperature are both affected by the nervous system when someone is anxious which is why people do this behavior when they're lying.

People also may scratch their neck or pull out the collar of their clothes when they're lying. This action helps the person to take some of their anxious energy and use it in a different way. If you see someone doing this while they're talking to you, there's a good chance that they are lying. They may be just itchy, but if they have no reason to be itchy or if they continue to do it excessively, they could be lying. This action helps the person to take some of their anxious energy and use it in a different way. If you see someone doing this while they are talking to you, there's a good chance that they are lying.

If the person reaches toward their eyes, or rubs their eyes repeatedly while speaking to you, it could be a subconscious sign that they are covering their eyes so as to not look at you. They may do this because they feel embarrassed that they are not telling the truth. We often times cover our eyes when we are embarrassed, so it makes sense that people would do the same when they're lying.

If the person talking to you hold their hand to their mouth or covers up their mouth while they are talking to you, it could also be a sign that they are lying. This is a primal instinct that people have since being young children. It comes from the primal instinct to cover up your mouth when you are saying something that you know you should not say. In this case, however, you do it subconsciously instead of on purpose. You may never even notice that you are doing it.

Even touching your nose can be a sign of lying. This is because touching the nose can be a form of comfort for many people; they may itch their nose or just briefly touch it. Either way, it could be a sign of lying if there is no reason for the person to actually be itchy.

Another way to tell if a person is lying is by looking at their body posture. Typically, if a person is lying, they will use what is called a closed body posture. This is made up of the person pulling their chin inward and their arms being held close to their body. And also include crossing of the legs and turn in the body away from the thing that they are nervous about. These are all supposed to make the body seem less intimidating which makes the person believe that their lie may be more believable.

The way that a person moves their eyes can also show that they are lying. If a person is not making much eye contact, it could be a direct signal that they are lying. On the other hand, excessive eye contact could mean that the person is trying really hard to look like they are telling the truth. That way, if eye contact does not seem typical, it could mean that the person is lying when they talk to you. Eyes that move back and forth quickly and look at many things around the room could also mean that a person is very nervous and

lying. If a person knows what they're doing and tries to avoid this behavior, they could actually stare at one thing for too long. Once again, if a person is using eyes that do not seem normal, it could mean that they're avoiding telling the truth.

In addition, when people are telling the truth, they generally look in one direction. Then, when they are lying, they will look in the opposite direction. This behavior has to do with the dominant brain hemisphere that individuals have. So, if a person is right-handed, they will look to the left when telling the truth. If they are left-handed, they will look to the right. While this is not a technique is not infallible, it is a great tip-off that someone is hiding something.

Other signs of body language that a person is lying could be signs that also show when a person is nervous. If a person is standing up and acting very fidgety, it could mean that they're lying. They may also look sweaty and breathe shallowly. Whether or not the signs are showing if a person is acting strange when they're talking to you it is important to understand that they may not be telling the truth. After reading the information in this chapter, you should be able to tell when the people around you are lying. You have been given many tools, and if you use them together, you will find the truth.

Thus, it is important to keep an eye on the subtleties of movement in your interlocutor. If you pay close attention, they might be letting on a lot more than you think. Consequently, you may find a lot more contextual clues to a person's behavior than you might have originally thought.

How To Use Body Language To Your Own Benefit

Now that we have covered all of the little details and learned a large amount about how to read body language, it's time to learn how to use this skill for your own benefit. After all, this is probably the reason why you bought this book and why you have been reading along this entire time.

First, let's look into how you can use body language to make friends. If you are attending social events often and hoping to make friends but it's just not really happening, knowing the body language that you are portraying as well as being able to read the body language of the people around you can be extremely helpful.

The first thing that you will need to do is make yourself look friendly and open to conversation. You will want to smile and make eye contact with the people around you. You will also want to make sure that you are standing with your body in an open stance with your feet at shoulder width apart.

Next, you'll need to look at the body language of the people around you. If someone is standing in a closed-off fashion or sitting with their head in their hands, they are probably not good options when looking for a person open to a new friendship. You will want to find someone with body language similar to what you are using yourself.

An extra tip to use once you start a conversation with a friendly person is to use your new skills in mirroring. If you smile when they smile and take on the body language that they present, you may be able to form a quick connection with that person. This may lead you to making a new friend in a way that was much simpler than you could have ever imagined.

Next, let's look at how you can use body language to find a new romantic partner. Finding someone to date is similar to making a new friend. You will want to make sure to use the same body language tools to allow yourself to appear open and inviting. In addition to the body language that we have gone over for friendship, you will want to add in some romantic features as well. You may want to stand with your chest pressed outward to show the people you are talking to that you are attractive. You may even want to gently touch the person when they are talking to show that you are interested in them. It also helps to laugh at their jokes as this shows interest as well.

You may someday need to use body language to succeed in the workplace. To do this, a good tool to use is Power Stances. You will want to look confident and trustworthy. Use the power body language to show that you are a capable leader who deserves to advance in their field.

We have looked at a few ways to use your own body language to benefit your life, but let's also look into how being able to read the body language of the people around you can help you in many ways as well.

First of all, if you can read body language you can often tell when a person is lying to you. If you suspect that the person you are conversing with is not telling the truth, you should watch to see what types of subtle movements their body is doing. Are they reaching up to touch their nose? Are they covering their mouth when they speak? Do they seem to be nervously fidgeting and tapping their toes? These could all be signs that the person is lying to you. They may also be lying if they are avoiding eye contact or making eye contact for too long in an attempt to cover up the falsehood of the facts they are stating.

You could also use body language—both reading it and manipulating your own—to save yourself from an uncomfortable position. Perhaps you are out at a bar with a friend and start talking with a stranger that approached you while you were both ordering drinks. You notice that this person is starting to

lean closer to you, open up their body by uncrossing their arms, their leg is touching yours, and their eyes even seem to dilate without any notable change in the lighting around you. From what you have learned in this book about body language, you suspect that they are interested in you beyond friendship. If you do not reciprocate these feelings, you can adjust your own body language to let them know without hurting their feelings. Lean away from them, cross your arms over your chest, avoid both touch contact and eye contact with them, etc. They should get the hint and hopefully move along. If they do not, you can also try manipulating your relational body language when around your friend to make it seem as though you are more than friends. If the other person sees you engaging in body language that implies a romantic relationship, they will probably back off. This advantage of reading and employing body language is particularly handy for women.

Furthermore, you might someday need to use body language as a defense in a dangerous situation. If someone is extremely upset with you, you can read their body language to be able to tell if they intend on hitting you or hurting you in any other way. Are they holding their arm behind their back with their other hand? This could mean that they are restraining themselves from punching you. Are they puffing out their chest? This might mean they are trying to intimidate you with their strength. With this knowledge, you will be able to decode body language in difficult situations so that you can protect yourself from violent occurrences or at least be ready when they are about to happen.

You might also be able to use body language to save someone else from an uncomfortable or even dangerous situation. It can be hard to believe until you are actually put into this position, but those of us who have been there know how hard it is to speak up or just walk away when stuck in an awkward or hazardous scenario—due to social conventions with the former and often threat of bodily harm with the latter. If a bystander can read body language, it could be a lifesaver for someone in such cases. I know this from personal experience.

When I was in my last year of college, I once went out with some friends to a very popular club near our university, just trying to have a good time and relax after our winter finals. It was Saturday night, so it was very busy, and we all dispersed to our own activities—dancing, drinking, chatting, flirting and subsequently striking out. After a few hours, we all agreed to meet up at the bar. When we got there, I noticed one of our female friends wasn't there. We took a quick look around and noticed her over by the wall with this guy who seemed to be hitting on her. She was smiling and laughing, so everyone assumed that everything was fine.

Still, something didn't seem right to me. I noticed that my friend kept crossing her arms over her chest and would stiffen every time this guy moved toward her. Her smile didn't reach her eyes, and her eyes seemed to be looking anywhere but at the guy talking to her. Based on her body language, she was obviously uncomfortable, and I decided to go check on her. The man left almost as soon as I came up to them and tried to introduce myself. My friend couldn't have been more relieved. She told me that the man had been following her around all night, grinding up on her, hitting on her, and in general just not leaving her alone. Not only that, but he had already hinted at her that he had a concealed carry, which made her scared to push him by rejecting him. Thanks to my ability to read her body language and catch on to her discomfort, my friend was saved from a potentially deadly situation.

At the end of the day, your ability to understand your own mannerisms and behaviors will enable you to communicate effectively and provide your interlocutors with the right message. After all, all languages, including body language, are intended to communicate meaning among people.

Reading the Body Language of A Child

We have already learned that body language can mean different things to people of different cultures, but did you know that reading the body language that is portrayed by children can also be a different experience? In this chapter, we will look into why a child's body language is different, how to read the body language of a child, and why this is an important thing for parents and guardians to know how to do.

First of all, we should talk about why it is different to read the body language of a child. The first reason is that they are young and have not yet learned to control their emotions. If a child is sad, they cry. If a child is happy, they smile. If they are angry, they yell and make mad faces, and if they are embarrassed, their cheeks turn red and they hide their face. Some children might even decide to tell you about the emotions that they are feeling. Children are new to the world and have no reason to hide the things that they are going through.

Because of this, children have body language that is extremely easy to read. They do not know how to control their emotions, so they always show how they feel. If you read the emotions of a child, you are reading what they truly feel.

Another important thing to note about reading the body language of children is that since they do not yet know how to hide their emotions, they also are unaware of the body language signs that they portray. They are not capable of sending the opposite signal of how they are feeling like adults are.

Their lack of awareness of their own body language can also make it easy to spot when a child is lying. A child might try to hide the truth through their words, but they do not have the wherewithal to think to conceal it in their body language as well, often allowing tells to slip through that they are not telling the truth or are omitting part of the truth.

For example, my sister has a five-year-old daughter who likes to sneak chocolate chip cookies before dinner. My sister always checks the Chips Ahoy package right before she starts making dinner, so she knows when a cookie is missing. She will still ask her daughter in the hopes that her daughter will confess on her own. Most of the time, my niece will try to lie about it (my personal favorite being when she claimed her father ate the cookie). However, no matter how convincing she might think she sounds, she has one big tell that she is lying: a huge smile plastered on her face. Because she thinks she is getting away with something so mischievous, this smile appears on her face as she is so proud of her deceit. When it is clear that she will not get away with it, this smile is usually replaced by another tell, i.e. her hanging her head while looking at the floor because she is ashamed at having been caught.

Everyone has their physical tell that gives them away when they are lying, and fortunately for parents, guardians, and teachers, children are unable to hide their tells until they are older and have more experience both with lying and with reading their own body language.

Now that we know how simple it is to read the body language of a child, let's look into how important it is to pay attention to the signals a child is conveying. Whether you are around children a lot or not, you need to be able to read a child's body language so that you can do your part in ensuring that our children are healthy and safe. Like reading an adult's body language can help us determine if they are in a dangerous situation, so can we also use a child's body language to determine if they are in any danger. The unfortunate truth is that we live in a world in which people will abuse, kidnap, and otherwise harm children. We want to be able to help children out of such situations, but it can often be hard to tell when something suspicious is actually going on.

Being able to read a child's body language can help us to determine if there is more to the situation than meets the eye. Because young children do not know how to control their body language, any discomfort they feel around a specific adult will manifest in such ways as how they hold themselves around this person. For instance, if a child exhibits such body language as standing stiffly, hunching their shoulders forward to make themselves smaller, or avoiding eye contact with everyone, including the adult they are with, it could mean that they are afraid of something. If they flinch whenever the adult that they are with reaches over to touch them, it could very well mean that this fear stems from someone hurting them on a regular basis, most likely this adult. Also, if they refuse to initiate physical contact with this adult while still never wandering any significant distance from them, it could mean that they are afraid to have any intimacy with this adult and of doing anything to anger them.

Mind you, none of this is a reason to call the police or Child Protective Services on someone. After all, there are multiple interpretations to any given body language. Standing stiffly, hunching their shoulders forward, or avoiding eye contact, for example, could just mean that the child is not comfortable in that particular environment or with strangers. Flinching and avoiding initiating physical contact with the adult could indicate, rather than fear, that the child has a problem with physical touch overall or that they are mad with that adult for some reason. Not wandering far from the adult even though it is natural for a child to want to explore could simply show that the child is well behaved or not particularly comfortable with checking out their surroundings on their own.

Like with all body language reading, what a child's body language means often depends on the context. If you know the child and/or adult personally, it can be easier to determine what the child's body language means. If they are complete strangers, it will be trickier. Nevertheless, spotting such body language in a child will help you to be on alert so that if suspicion arises that the child is being abused or has been kidnapped, you will be ready to take action.

Reading a child's body language will also help you to be there for them emotionally. If you have a child or take care of a child for large amounts of time, they will consider you their support system. They need you to help them learn about their lives and the world around them. This includes learning how to handle their emotions.

Sometimes, a child might have an emotion that they do not yet know how to explain. They may express this feeling through body language but still feel frustrated when they are unable to put their experience into words.

As an adult who knows how to read body language, you can help in this situation. You can read the nonverbal cues that the child is portraying and use them to help the child express his or her feelings verbally. This will help the child to learn about their feelings and more about who they are as a person. It will also help the child to grow up knowing that feelings are healthy and that it is okay to share your struggles with the people who are close to you. If you can help your child in this way and teach these things to your child at a young age, they will have significantly fewer emotional struggles over the course of their life. This understanding is important to any adult who deals with children such as doctors, teachers and parents dealing with other kids such as their children's friends.

It is not only important for parents and caregivers to teach their children about how to express their own body language, but it is important for them to teach the kids about simple body language reading techniques as well. You might not want to call it body language reading to them because they either will not understand or will think the topic is boring, but it is important that this skill be taught to children in whatever creative way necessary.

You might wonder why I believe it is important for children to be able to read body language, since it is a science-based topic that can be complicated at times. We will explain why this is important now.

First, if your children understand that nonverbal communication has just as much meaning as the words that they speak, they will be able to understand the people around them at a new level. Take their time on the playground, for example. If they ask a friend to play with them and the friend says no but is looking at the ground and has another child staring at them as if to tell them not to go play with the child, they will know that there is more meaning behind this situation. They will either be able to speak up for their friend and encourage them to do what they want without worrying about what other people think, or they will be able to walk away without feeling offended because they know that there was more to the conversation than a simple denied request to play. In fact, this might even be a sign that the friend was bullied away from playing and your child will be able to tell a trusted adult what they saw.

Also, think about if your child sees a classmate that is not saying much when they usually talk all day, every day. If your child is aware of the body language of the people around them, they might notice this difference in behavior and ask the child what is wrong. This could make a huge difference in the sad child's day.

You might even consider the friendships that the child already has. You know that as an adult, being able to read simple body languages allows you to have better friendships. It makes sense, then, that the same is true with friendships among children.

Your child will also be able to avoid being a bully better if they are aware of their own body language. They will understand that actions like rolling of the eyes or walking away from someone when they are talking to them hurts just as much as mean words. They will be able to understand these actions and avoid them in order to be nice to the people around them when other children might accidentally hurt their friends with actions like these without knowing the consequences.

When a child knows body language, they are able to make sure that their friends are comfortable with them. If the child sits close to a friend, they will be able to tell if the friend is okay with the close contact or not. If the friend is not okay with it and is showing signs of being uncomfortable, the child will know that the right thing to do is move away.

A lot of these types of body language are things that children learn through real-life experience. The only problem with this is if they are learning in real life, then real feelings are getting hurt, and real friends are feeling uncomfortable. The sooner a child learns these skills, the sooner they can use body language to their advantage. This is why it can be helpful to teach children about body language from a young age.

One way that you can teach body language to young children is by expressing how you feel out loud when you realize you are expressing something through body language. You could say, "I am shaking my head from side to side because I do not like what you are doing." You could also say, "I am smiling because I am happy to see you this morning."

You can use the same tactic to teach children about how their own body language affects the people around them. You could say, "I feel loved when you look at my eyes while I talk." You could also say, "When you walk away from me while I am talking to you, it makes me feel sad."

With these tools, you should be able to understand the body language that children present. You should also be able to see the importance of teaching body language to young children.

Conclusion

Now, we are here at the end of this book. We covered a lot of ground with regard to non-verbal communication and how this can enable you to read people. You can confidently put these ideas into practice.

Now that we have given body language serious consideration, it is up to you to put these new concepts into practice. After all, what good is all this knowledge if you can't put it to good use?

Becoming a master communicator is a lot easier than you think. However, it takes some good, old-fashioned elbow grease. Please take the time to go over any of the parts of this book that you feel you need to review and then get out there and make the most of them. You will find that when you are able to read people effectively, you will be able to communicate with them on a deeper, more meaningful level. This will enable you to gain people's confidence and thereby become a more confident individual.